The Garden of

Fragile

Beings

poems by

Carolyn Welch

Finishing Line Press
Georgetown, Kentucky

The Garden of

Fragile

Beings

Copyright © 2018 by Carolyn Welch
ISBN 978-1-63534-736-4 First Edition
All rights reserved under International and Pan-American Copyright Conventions.
No part of this book may be reproduced in any manner whatsoever without written permission from the publisher, except in the case of brief quotations embodied in critical articles and reviews.

ACKNOWLEDGMENTS

Some poems have appeared or are forthcoming in the following publications under the name Carolyn Welch Scarbrough:

Connecticut River Review: "Hematology Clinic"
Poet Lore: "Traffic"
Tar River Poetry: "Thinking of Mom Smoking" (reprinted in anniversary edition)
SUNDOG The Southeast Review: "Nurse"
High Desert Journal: "On Writing"
Cyber Collaboration "Writings from the Bennington Collective: "Aftermath, Revisited,"
    "Donald Hall Reading Jane Kenyon," "Nurses In Spring," "September's Baby" (as
    "September"), "The Way the Baby Wakes."
The Minnesota Review: "Nurses In Spring"
Frostwriting: "Rain Run," "Writing Exercise," "Peonies," "Monday Morning," "Art of
    Respiration," "It's True About Owls," "Valentine's Day Reminder"
American Journal of Nursing: "A Rose by Any Other Name"
Bellevue Literary Review: "Gone" (Editor's Choice selection)
Kore Press Anthology, "Girls"

Publisher: Leah Maines

Editor: Christen Kincaid

Cover Art and Design: Jeffery P. Bailey

Author Photo: Jeffery P. Bailey

Printed in the USA on acid-free paper.
Order online: www.finishinglinepress.com
         also available on amazon.com

Author inquiries and mail orders:
Finishing Line Press
P. O. Box 1626
Georgetown, Kentucky 40324
U. S. A.

Table of Contents

Nurses in Spring 1
After Irises 2
Hematology Clinic 3
Monday Morning 4
Watershed 5
In the Garden of Fragile Beings 6
Aftermath, Revisited 7
The Relinquishing, Day One 8
Child 9
Traffic 10
It's True About Owls 11
Missing 12
Evidence 13
Peonies 14
All of These Things 15
Writing Exercise 16
Despite The Cloudy Morning 17
Rain Translation 18
Waiting 19
Art of Respiration 20
Love Poem 21
This Time 22
Nurse 23
Pediatric Transport #689 24
Bulldozers in June 25
Fifteenth Anniversary Poem 26
Love Stories 27
Girls 28
On Writing 29
A Rose By Any Other Name 30
Metaphor 31
Brief History of August 32
August, Pressing In 33
The End, Or Maybe Not 34
August Swimmer 35
Last Rites 36
A Lamentation Of Grass 37

Roses In September 38
Two-Year Olds in ICU 39
Ladybird 40
Eurydice And Orpheus, After A Separation 41
Donald Hall Reading Jane Kenyon 42
Thinking of Mom Smoking 43
Gone 44
A Way Out 45
Of Rocks, Soil, These Grasses 46
The Living 47
Girl, Frowning 48
How To Know When It's Over 49
The Garden of Fragile Metaphors 50
After Snow 51
January 52
Rain Run 53
Rose of Sharon 54
Just Checking 55
Brain Death Established: 3:07 P.M. 56
ICU Nurses 57
Daughter, Sleeping 58
Valentine's Day Reminder 59
The Winter Side of Spring 61
An Hour Lacking Complex Emotions 62
Things That Are Absurd 63
Update to Dad 65
Note to Heart 66
Thirst 67
Happy Dog Poem 68
Late Spring 69
Understanding 70
Error 71
Last Sunday of May, Pediatric I.C.U. 72
Hospital Smoker 73
Mercy 74
Lyme Disease 75
Two Walls Painted 76

For my Mom, of course, for everything.

And for my fellow nurses working in the trenches, doing what I will always consider to be the most important and hardest work.

Nurses in Spring

There is a pause and the conversation turns
and we try to name the deaths so far this year.

The windows here are thick, industrial strength
and all we know of the season
is the glare of blue sky
and the silent blooming of pear trees
four stories down

and a few feet farther, the white petals
rain tore free and dropped
a few hours ago.

After Irises

The irises left husks
topped with small trumpets of brown.
They clatter in wind like old sorrows
knocking.

When I tug firm and steady
the stalks snap clean from the ground
as if they were meant to break
this very way.

Hematology Clinic

This girl who instructs me is eight, a new floppy hat
on her bald head and a flowered dress. She likes dressing up,
knows the long names of her medications and is an authority
on how I should tape the needle and with which bandage.

She has learned that this is how we live. Naming things.
Acute Myeloblastic Leukemia, Vincristine, Methotrexate.
Marking our places with numbers. White blood counts,
lymph counts, platelets counts.

When she is a brat, we tell her mother to enforce the rules,
the same as before. So she knows this too:
that this insistence on order is a manner of not dying.
We teach her to count, to pronounce, to behave.

Monday Morning

I read a poem by a woman who
writes that death enters her room, tells her
she will only write about him.
As if any collection of words fails to
bear him along; any sky, any
yawning hour of night, any river,
ocean or even this simple stream of
water twisting down the bathroom
drain, braided with incandescent light;
light that reveals every line,
every mark of fatigue, every living
pore. Death is there like a lover, like
a god, like the pungent odor
at low tide, the tartness left on
the tongue after blueberries,
after every sweetness.

Watershed

The swollen creek strains through
convoluted narrows, around upturned trees and
boulders, sieves through branch-clogged tributaries and turns
to the wide relief of the Clinch.
There is a basement dark room in
my heart. You are there
and so am I, blood churning
through and around the lowly room, like a barely
noticed eddy in the river, practically unknown
except for a small leeching from the whole,
this limping along way of loving.
The heart's doors flap open, snap closed
thousands of times an hour, this hour,
the last hour and the next—open
close, open, like flood gates trying to
control damage, as if damage were not a part
of the whole story.

In the Garden of Fragile Beings

Alarms demand this and that, a
frustrated father is at the desk, someone
wants coffee, one mother fails to show up
for her crying child, another needs to
let go because this one is going
no matter how many times we try
to not let her. They are all here

lying in mechanical beds, sitting disheveled
in uncomfortable chairs, in gowns
that allow a patch of skin, a bony knee, a cannulated
wrist, a thick catheter taped to a leg.
One girl smiles, head heavy
with bandages, another child cries
and in the room I enter, a man and woman are
tender with the post-op boy, faces kind
and haunted with possibility. Here

thresholds of all sorts press in
and I yearn for simple things—for my failing irises
and tight-fisted hot pink peonies, rain drenched
beds vigorous with weeds, waiting;
a hemlock laden with spring-
greened tips. My eyes are famished for

everything that speaks of the trivial place
where a few days ago, one daughter tugged loose
a thick peony stem, then flung it away because
it crawled with ants and another daughter
took it up, placed it in a glass of water.

Aftermath, Revisited

Why does the storm-pummeled garden
with leaves and petals scattered and dirtied,

yet lovely (like the word ravished), remind me
of glass shattered all over the highway

and the snarl of wreckage that straightened
our road-weary backs and clinked

in our bellies
as we drove past? The storm's aftermath

and the human wreckage lure us
the way the word does—Ravish—

which is not only a force that gently overtakes
such as physical beauty, but the taking of

that which was, moments ago, vital, beating, or simply
lovely. The smashed peonies, for instance,

or the bruise that remembers
some pressing force,

the continual giving
and taking away.

The Relinquishing, Day One

You were that blue, lanugo-coated ball of human
unfolding between my knees, and I was the body bent over,
assuring myself the whole of you was correctly arranged.

While you and I were still coated with the mess of our splitting,
the pain already a token I knew I would want,
I watched you move the way I'd felt you move—

your hip that curved the right side of my belly lopsided,
heels that punched at the boundary of my liver.
Then, this relinquishing.

I think of Thetis allowing Achilles his human life—
the goddess only a mother, after all. Then,
I stood by. I let them wipe me from you, let them diaper

your new body, let them band a name around an ankle,
and wrap you into what was then called newborn.
Then, even I took you, declared you, my son, my Logan.

Child

You, my sweetbitter unmanageable
creature, who steals nightly into my bed
claiming whatever desire the years have
named upon the center, ravishing our sheets this way
and that, so I wake to an ankle across my breast
see your sleep-flushed cheek on your father's
upper arm, memory of my own cheek
on that same arm, and yet I cannot
displace you and he cannot and we
tangle nightly in darkness or, like tonight, in
a spill of moonlight until you settle, splayed like
some crooked-armed star drawn
atop a tree in expectation of
all good things.

from Sappho fragment "…sweetbitter unmanageable creature who steals in…"

Traffic

Of the two cars in front of us, the first pokes along,
brakes lighting at each scenic opening between trees,
taking curves at a pace sure not to disturb the coffee
in the sturdy mug on the dash.

And the second rides the bumper of the first,
weaves right, center, left, center, trying to pester
the other driver into checking any of three mirrors.

They are like that place near the end of love,
that place where one lover still believes.

It's True About Owls

The silent flight of their hollow boned, soft-
feathered bodies. This one
has switched perches to observe me
as I exit the woods, the movement
sudden and silent like the change from love
to indifference
and back again, the flight itself
imperceptible.
You were here, now there
and it's unfathomable
I never heard a thing.

Missing

There is no post-tornado pile of
splintered boards, but simply an entire house
missing from the neighborhood, as if someone had
leaned over and carefully removed it
from a game, leaving flower beds and sidewalks
undisturbed around a blank rectangle.
The other homes, unscathed
and in their places, go on as usual.

It is like the one car in the traffic jam
in which a woman is sobbing.

Evidence

We turn the child's body side to side,
one of us holding the chart next to bruises to
determine their age. Then photographs
and swabbing for other evidence. Eventually

we retreat to the lounge, guiltily hungry
and wrung-out. One by one we enter
the sanctuary of lunch chatter, pass silly,
tactless offerings around the formica table

until we each have partaken, each entered
this refuge.

Peonies

Last week, their bulbous buds were
fisted tight and now their extravagance drags
across the sidewalk and dirt, sweetness
riddled with ants. At night the fresh-waxed
cars of prom-going teens pass by, girls
in lavish dresses that will brush all night over
thresholds and the tops of boyfriends'
shoes. The weight of ripeness, the living as if
it's all a feast, then these soiled tattered petals

which remind me of a remarkable elderly woman
brushing a hair behind her ear, lovely still and strong
still, but underneath, biology shredding the strong heart,
the quick mind.

All night the boys drive by, calculating
how to remove expensive dresses that the girls'
bodies are unaccustomed to. The girls submit to
the evening gowns, every move accompanied by odd pullings,
rubs and rustles, the gowns altering everyday movements—

the careful car exit, the required lift to climb stairs, the simple lack
of a pocket or comfortable shoes. Do they see my young
girls watching and pointing excitedly?

They are princesses, the happily ever-afters
driving by in freshly waxed cars with boys in ties
and tuxedos. In our yard, my own daughters
are drawn to the statuesque iris,
the shouty tulips, and I must lead them

to the peonies, raise the ant infested heads
to their noses and see their surprise as
they inhale again and again.

All of These Things

We danced, my feet on top of my father's.
There was laughter
and our feet dancing

and all of the things he was not that night
and my pretty mother
not looking unhappy.

Writing Exercise

The exercise is simple:
a first word and another word and so on.
Most become only scaffolding into
the *real* poem, the opening
knocked away, the way some
topple first marriages and others
our one marriage again and again

and how are we to know, finally, which is
the meant life, the yes in
a sea of broken things?

Despite The Cloudy Morning

It comes, despite the chill damp
and the lone small-voiced bird under
a window in suburbia
or the woodpecker
at his pecking in the barren wood
or the wind wafting in with
predictions of rain and cold.
Nearly imperceptible greens come
as wisps on a neighbor's willow, moss
between stones and beginning
on the tree trunk that has clung to
this same hillside for years; coming
on slowly, like the forgiveness
I thought would never enter me
though I beckoned it. Maybe,
it's like that tree clinging to the hillside
in some unspoken pact with gravity
an outcome unforced, unbidden
and true.

Rain Translation

It's the sort of rain that says
you should be in the forest,

squatting in a cave's mouth
trying to comprehend the trickles

and drums and in-between notes
for the music does what all great music

does—names what we are:
Sorrow, longing, hope.

Rain presses down and relents
says yes it's true. All of it true.

Believe everything.

Believe evening light
firing the weeds

and also the stubby grass returning.
Believe the bloody birth

and your own hands upon the newborn
claiming every surface.

Believe the gunshot wound festering the belly
of a boy who means to die.

Believe you are the loved newborn
and also the boy.

Believe rain will deliver you safely
from its translation of yesterday.

There is no other choice
but this one.

Waiting

The hummingbird is at the feeder,
poised as if motionless, green-backed by
the container of sugared red water,
wings beating invisibly fast.

The heart is a flight of notes
beneath a husk of ribs and feathers.

Art of Respiration

When the call came the car was on empty,
I was late, stopping for gas and
no one in front of me moving fast
enough. The cashier looked at
my scrubs, my badge as I shoved
money toward her, trying to hurry and
go. She said, my boyfriend died, died
right in front of me and I told him
I loved him. Do you think he heard?
Yes, I said, and slowed down, told her
what I know and
it was a little like breathing,
me giving her this true thing and she needing it,
taking it in like air.

Love Poem

> *No one contradicts me now and the salt has gone out of my life*
> —Queen Victoria, after Albert's death

Do you know the body knows you're
going to move before you know? That the motor
cortex begins an action before you think of
doing it? That the body begins to react before
you even know you've seen something to react to?
Maybe this has nothing to do with love,

nothing to do with why we say the things we say
or why we don't quit when others might have quit.
No therapist has told us that something incomprehensible,
something animal inside us, binds us
keeps us coming together, despite other
logic, other ways of failing

This Time

Last night, my dream, our father swimming,
not drowning in Monday night football, six o'clock news,
and unmanageable saliva. But leaving again.

We watched each gaunt arm stroke,
saw knobs of shoulders roll under and through
and the frail body moving into blue and

this time we knew what we could not ask.
We let him go to the water which possessed him,
let it claim the skin and vein that hold life in

and this time we were not greedy children.
We allowed him to possess
the salty body of his own grief.

Nurse

1. Surgery

It is like a hunger, this watching.
A body is opened and observed in its living.
The organs go strangely on about their jobs
despite this entering.

It is like watching dying,
the way it is suddenly done—
the slice into a shock of reds
and how the viewing is like betrayal.

2. Isolation

I am a voyeur, whether I mean to be or not.
Today it is the rain from a sheltered porch—
three walls solid around me, a roof overhead
and a faltering wall of rain in front.

Yesterday, it was a sickness and a baby
and my friend Grace saying come in and look
and telling me the story and both of us staring,
saying *my god*.

Pediatric Transport #689

It is dark and rainy as it should be.
In the back of the ambulance,
we complain about our driver
who swerves too much and mashes the brakes

and cannot hear us. She cannot hear us,
our young driver who looks bewildered
as she stares intently into the small place
the headlights allow.

One of us suctions mucous from the boy.
Another squeezes air from the bag into his lungs
twenty times a minute. The woman next to me
calls out numbers I write in the record.

We chat and laugh a little in the spaces
between tasks, like women who are comfortable
together. We continue, though he cannot live
and we should've been home hours ago.

Bulldozers in June

The tangle of conversation
snares us into silence.
Outside is the hum of undoing as
bulldozers clear the woods and

the breakage of trees enters
our lack—the crack and snap and
splitting of every sort of tree.
And for the young couple

planning their new home
this cleared place is
something other than
the wound we see.

Fifteenth Anniversary Poem

> *June 15, 2000*

The female cardinal flits tree to tree
from one end of the wood to the other.
And he is one branch behind
always.

I think it a courtship, the way he pursues her,
then see twigs clutched in their beaks and realize
they are not new to one another.
They are the same pair I've seen every year

and still he finds his way
to each of her branches and still she moves
confidently through the wood to the place
they have made, are making.

Love Stories

And here we are,
the consolation of rain
and our field of loneliness,
one void leads
to the next. The rain steady,
the spaces between droplets
palpable like the children
between us, almost filling
what the rain calls to
as it drenches the thirsting
garden, finds the fissures
to the very roots
and would you understand
now why I cry
during love stories?

Girls

If I could go back to me
in the neighbor's yard, on a late evening in summer,
minutes before dark, I'd return to the game of
Smear the Queer played with my girlfriends and their
brothers and brothers' friends, return to
being chased and tackled and piled upon by
all the other players, grass staining my knees
and the skin of my elbows, back to one particular
game when one boy tackled me again and again
his two hands grabbing my two new breasts
flinging me to the ground, holding on too long
and I pretended not to notice for tackle after tackle
but finally turned and yelled at him to stop
and he did. I'd go back and say to the girl me
never hesitate like that, and I wouldn't have
again and again all those next years.
We played all summer, but with this new knowledge
that ruined everything and summer nights
were never again about grass and fireflies
and mothers calling us home.

On Writing

Today it is the crows who speak.
They must be speaking about wind
relieving the heat a bit
or about the lake's water level
having dropped.

Maybe one has lost a child
and she is rousing the others
so that there are two groups cawing
first from one tree, then another,
trying to lure the small thing home.

A Rose By Any Other Name

It blooms white on the CT scan—
small fist, opaque rose, unfurling where
the vessel is shorn inside
the infant's brain.

I look from images, white with breakage in
wrong places, evidence of violent acts,
to the father—only a boy really, eyes dark-circled
and weary and it is easier to believe

almost anything else. I think
of shriveled spheres of red-black petals
saved in a jar when I was a girl
now aged to the color of old blood.

Why must I move from injury to roses;
trauma to love, my mind
unhanding one for the other as if good
cancels this, metaphor necessary

like religion. Still, this rose, this white
wrongness in the frontal lobe, will take him,
once the swelling begins and I have written of flowers
instead of weeping.

Metaphor

He is beating the dead horse.
But is the horse dead from the beating
or did he find the horse lying motionless
and desire to rouse it with blows?

Does he know it is dead?
Does he want it to get up?
Is he enthralled by his violence?
Does he love the animal?

Brief History of August

The butterfly bush trembles with swallowtails and monarchs
and Sarah says they come because
she loves them.

Maybe it's like that. Maybe if we love well enough,
if we believe like a four year old believes,
desire will sustain us.

Today, on the bush near the house, a cluster of swallowtails
is frenzied upon the final flowers.
They cling to the blooms, circle and probe,

wings ragged with wear, circle and probe
and the bush quivers with their weight and movements,
until it doesn't.

Last night the movie was a love story.
I want to tell you how the movie and the butterflies
help me love you. But I don't.

After the movie I slip my leg over yours,
my foot over your foot and our bodies are
a season unfolding

and the tears that come after
are not about the movie or our bodies greedy for each other
or they are about both

and about the trembling bushes that whisper
don't go
as everything goes.

August, Pressing In

>   "*…emptiness has its own way of going.*"   —Liam Rector

It's August. Drought has opened fissures on
the tomatoes. Pulp leaks out, glossy like
the marrow of ruined bones. Some shrivel and rot and

some go on with it. We, who think we know
you, circle around your death,
study what we think about it.

I found a paper that would annoy you, examining
pronoun usage by suicidal poets and thought
what a waste—of time, I mean.

Bright orange cosmos crowd the garden paths,
refuse yet, to be any sort of dark metaphor.
We remain in this fallen world

and speak of how your death affects us.
If my father had asked for too much Morphine,
I'd have given it to him.

The scent of basil permeates the yard.
As soon as I step outside, it hits me—
it's the beginning of the end now,

basil bitterer by the day, blossoms holding nothing
back, cold metal in your hands, the cold
deliberation. There is only so much to talk about.

It's August and cicadas are fairly screaming
with the lateness of the season, the press of the end
all around us.

The golden hues of thriving cosmos and marigolds merge
with those of dying grass and failing leaves and fade into evening
like good and proper things.

The End, Or Maybe Not

Here at the end of things
the heroes embrace
as the volcano explodes

for what turns out to be
not the end yet, but a commercial
break. The movie keeps going,

seems to end four more times.
Surely, no audience can crank out
the required amount of emotion

for which each non-ending begs.
Surely we can't keep talking
of your death. We are weary

with it, yet no one says:
He's done it. He's gone.

August Swimmer

The pool was a fifty meter plain of unbroken blue, smooth
and empty and lit by early morning sun.
I was sixteen. In four months I'd meet my future husband
for the first time. In August,

the water held an accrual of summer heat,
stored days bound like vague memories of a time before
a memorable event; like the long days themselves
of rising at five a.m., of swimming unremarkable lap
after unremarkable lap that left our muscles
satisfied and exhausted. In August,

the water achieved that temperature
compatible with the body's, so diving in lacked
the usual shock. The silky water simply received us.
And whether the race was smooth and quick
or a long desynchronized affair, the water was like a dream
that at once held us back and let us go.

Last Rites

Rain grants its patient reprieve, as if
we hadn't been waiting
all summer. It won't touch us

enough, our hungry lawns and parched
garden plots, unreachable.
Should we now say:

hallowed be thy name and
forgive us and thanks, after
the night's rain? Zinnias

have collapsed. Cosmos, bright cheerleaders
through drought and failure, have failed.
The fat peppers remain unscathed

next to the sad roses, which are not ailing in
any particular manner, but continue
their eternal fall.

How to end the poem about ending?
It's raining. A soft steady drizzle
and we are all out in it.

A Lamentation Of Grass

—from Lucille Clifton's "grief."

Trees weep last night's rain
all over the lawn
whenever wind allows.

There is no agreement to grieve,
no discussion to end mourning.
Our lamentation is like

those narrow strips of grass placed
between rows of asphalt parking spaces,
an offering never spoken, never accepted.

Roses In September

I go out to the garden, see
what remains of them—hollowed

cusps of numbered petals
small testimonies to beauty,

to loss, to the drawn out departure
that says when we go, we should be

used up with living. Here is
the artful patience of leaving—

like a lover, desired, though departing
and saturated with want.

Two-Year Olds in ICU

They are the hardest to keep down with
the usual meds, will yank out the
very tubes they need, but

we love their firecracker
spirits. We smile, assure families
that flailing kicking rage is

a wonderful thing. The ones who
break us no longer bother. Today,
this small enraged boy takes

a huge breath as I suction his mouth
and remove the breathing tube.
Then tells me to get my hands off him.

Ladybird

> *Ladybird, ladybird, fly away home.*
>   *Your house is on fire, your children alone.*

Until this banishment you refuse
to call this house *home*.

Now you call home
the place you cannot enter.

We meet at the neutral place
to exchange our child

and my heart remembers
something.

This swapping of a child in silence
is homelessness.

I take the heart with me and he
chatters all the way about pumpkins and candy.

Eurydice And Orpheus, After A Separation

Orpheus has come to claim his wife, does not fathom
her departure or know his unknowing of this woman.

She cannot remember the familiarity of being wife,
yet walks behind the men, shroud-clad and dutiful.

She is patient, knows well her husband,
his lover's impatience and pities him what will come,

even as she desires what will come. She
has grown steadfast and unhurried

in afterlife, waits for Hermes to move between her
and the man who claims her, waits for the declaration

that Orpheus has disobeyed, has turned to see.
Her death clothes swirl as she turns away

and he does not see as she goes, her composure,
how her body moves with purpose.

Donald Hall Reading Jane Kenyon

Bennington College, 1997

He reads her poem before his own, their old
ritual. He leaves a sigh after her name; that sigh—
a small poem, unspeakable.

He reads of Jane watching him from a window above a sink
or from a back porch where the door surely creaks
before it smacks shut. She watches his cigarette burn

through a field of New Hampshire evening as he
completes the haying. And there, she sees
among grass and ember and labor

contentment and sorrow bound, one to the other.
He flips to the next poem, smiling, as if pleased
to find himself exactly here.

Thinking of Mom Smoking

The tree that leans so far
that I know it will not live a long life
has narrow leaves that divide and separate the light
and allow a quivering patchwork of shadows
to move slowly across the grass
until evening takes them.

The tree is leaning to the point
that our wagers now are on gravity to win.
Though not today. Today
there is strength enough to maintain
the difficult pose and there is a solid root mass
dug in, holding.

Gone

William's letter uses *suicided* as a verb
and really why not? The finite action

verb—without an introduction, unreduced by
other verbs, other introductory phrases

there on the page like the remaining sad facts—
the widow, the father…you know what all I mean

the *whys* and *what ifs* and *if only I'd knowns*
mowed down like a failing meadow in

October, fodder now for other animals,
something dry to chew on

all winter long.

A Way Out

The cardinal
who has worried the window panes for years
is gone.

No explanation,
no scattering of scarlet feathers
on the lawn.

I last saw him flitting through the trees
behind his mate,
mouth stuffed with pine needles.

How far will one branch after another take him
after years of fighting himself in the windows?

What of the rival
who stubbornly reappeared
each sunrise?

What made him turn and notice
how the branches make
a way out?

Of Rocks, Soil, These Grasses

The morning is steeped in dew
and between blades of young grass
the straw recedes into saturated ground.

Our son works among the blades, dislodges rocks,
studying their shapes in his palm.
He is nearly two and attentive to what can be held

and let go, picked up, put down.
He finds a keeper, encloses it in a fist,
moves on, unmindful of the shine of everything,

of how water soaks his shoes, how it enters
and overtakes the canvas fibers.
He is young enough that rocks, soil, these grasses

are at once treasures and expendable.
He unfists one for another
as easily as he moves without sorrow

another year from his beginning,
another closer to mindfulness and the leaving
of all that holds him in this lawn.

The Living

The sun flooding in
should be some final dazzling

event. Seeing the boy's father
weeping over the hospital bed

should be an end. None of us
should go on like we do.

Girl, Frowning

She is unaware of these past weeks,
of my intimate knowledge of her ill body,
her rashes and fevers, blood counts and
vital signs or how her mother and I
wanted to bathe her and brush her hair,
but she was too sick for even this.
All day I've removed tubes and old bandages
and now she sits, exhausted, in a chair.
We've washed and combed her bed-matted hair
and she has fussed and whined the whole
time. I smile at her clean pigtails and
she shoots me the worst frown
she can muster. I lean over her, say
grumpiness means you're getting better you know
and she works her hardest to keep at it.

How To Know When It's Over

My fresh anti-virus software is making the computer sick.
It's the same old story—the desire for safety
wrecking what had been a perfectly acceptable
working relationship. The insides churn away

my seconds, then minutes and I pray open, open
and eventually the file does open, but
without the old snap; more like a laborious
grind. Always the memory is

a mismatch—too much, too little.
The therapist says, the key to a long marriage
is a short memory. The technical support voice
in India says, buy more memory.

The Garden of Fragile Metaphors

I've chopped the finished stalks,
layered them in the compost pile
with leaves and cut grass, eggshells,
carrot peelings and fireplace ash.
There is heat down in there, where
decomposition is going just right, the
refuse black and loamy. Up here,
it's still bright fall—

zinnias and chrysanthemums and brilliant
oak leaves. I pitchfork the deep black material
over the green and yellow cuttings that here,
now, in this pile, are death. Here, now
it is darkness that seethes with heat.

After Snow

The baby, ill for two weeks, recovers.
The mother, awake for two weeks, sleeps.
When she wakes

a finch is at the bluebird's door.
A little snow is left and the sun
returns to the woods, hunting it.

January

In summer
we didn't speak of flowers
being gone

or winter thin woods.
Now, the lean of a tree speaks
of its end.

Chipped lichen, damaged bark,
the hard edge of sunlight
deep in a shady place.

The mother who
refuses to mourn until
there is no alternative.

Rain Run

I run and rain is pouring.
My shoes squish squish and ahead
my dog Bob turns to see if I'm coming
and continues on. I like being surrounded
by indifferent rain, by my own carrying on
through the forest. I've waited for
love to settle back over me
the way the noisy flock of crows settles
unexpectantly into the trees and grows silent, the way
pouring rain becomes its own room. If only
I could out run the hard edge of love, enter
the other side as I'll enter the warm house
and my children's voices will pepper me with
mom this and *mom that* like finches
flitting to the feeder again and again
and I'll forgive every childish transgression
that weighs upon motherhood and gather
the bright flames of them to me.

Rose of Sharon

Every two weeks I came home, tried not to look at
my father's failing body. When he pled for a massage
of muscles fatigued with the labor of breath

I flinched from the shock of ribs, the strain of skin
over each bone; hesitated by the pale wreckage
that refused to let me remain as child, as taker.

Unable to find a way out,
I rubbed, tried not to hear my own father moan
like an old dog being scratched.

In the car I read *The Grapes of Wrath*,
read of a teenage mother to a stillborn, breasts
milk sore and throbbing

and of the starving vacant-eyed man—his leathery
lips and whiskered face. She's told to feed him
and she does in the cold thankless camp.

Just Checking

Mom calls, asks about the kids
and what the doctor said.

One ear infection, one sinusitis.
She wants details.

She doesn't say *I'm getting old*
or *you're almost forty.*

She says if I need help on Tuesday
she can watch the baby.

She doesn't say *there is much to fear*
and I don't tell her I'm afraid already.

Brain Death Established: 3:07 P.M.

We are knowledgeable and adept at proving
the obvious; spend forty-five minutes turning off
non-essential electrical devices.
The EEG, unable to locate brain electricity,
finds voltage everywhere else. After
pronouncement, after removal,
we stand staring like the dumb animals
we keep forgetting we are; staring at
one of our own so obviously gone.

ICU Nurses

Our wingless salty hearts
plead to miss, at least today,
the trustworthy melancholy train.
Brakes squeal, doors fly open
and sarcasm leaps from our grieved
mouths. Where is

the bellwether of hope these southern
ministers go on about at bedsides of
children we call the *spinal mass* or
new-onset AML. If only, for one day,
the phone wasn't demanding space
for the next thing waiting.

Daughter, Sleeping

I step into a wood after a snowfall,
light multiplied by every surface.

Ice clinks in a hint of wind. The ache
of wind on cheek and forehead is

sweet and precise like the blade of snow
perched on a branch against the blue.

Valentine's Day Reminder

We've had a lot of years. Still, I do not want
some forlorn, sarcastic, let's ignore Valentines Day

day. Nor do I want the fat ballooning greeting card hearts on
every surface kind of love.

Give me this hula-hooping love that rises and falls,
spins its tediously annoying beads one day

and crashes to the floor on others.
Some may not think this is so amazing.

Lets face it—tonight is the coldest night of the year,
the children treat our bedroom like a train station

coming in when we want them to go,
forgetting their stuff when they leave.

Our cozy king size bed is littered with cracker crumbs, a
stuffed dog and a book about bugs. This

is the place they come to cry or vomit or wedge in
between us in the dread of night.

Outside, the moon is like a streetlight shining over
the dormant garden. Compost warms the bed

that held the lettuce that thrived, just as we left for
vacation. So we gave it all away.

Sometimes, we can't even speak. Sometimes
we laugh during sex. It's night. The electric blanket

has the bed just right. Someone knows, she's banging
at the door. We have something she wants. We

keep forgetting that what she wants is right here—

though we give it away and away
and yet it is here, knocking, knocking.

Winter Side of Spring

Hopes I hadn't dared welled up
along with daffodil and crocus buds

now frozen under a sky blue with
fair intentions. I watch the news.

I stand and stretch and see your eyes
light where my shirt bares my waist

and we temper desire by arguing the weekly
schedule—who should drive whom where,

irritation and desire shackled by
so much weather between us.

An Hour Lacking Complex Emotions

The sky is cold, puffed gray with chances of snow,
My hands, warm from laundry folding, hold the pen
with nothing more complex than happiness.

Sometimes, we come to knowing, or what feels like knowing,
or it comes upon us, for no reason, like today.
For a while we stay. We allow it to matter.

I revise the poem and its origins fall away.
It becomes like memory, allows the mediocre to fall away.
What remains is history, what we want to be, meant to be.

Things That Are Absurd

1.

I thought she was going to say *stroke*.
My mother said, *slurred speech.* She said,
Do you know how you're father's speech has been slurred lately?

They were moving to a condo. We were called home
to claim furniture, old report cards, a weed eater. *Where is he?*
I thought he might be dead already. I had not noticed (the speech).

All night I read reports—*slurred speech, right arm weakness,*
tongue fasciculations. They are *sad to diagnose.*
I claimed my old bed, the oak table, a collection of rocks.

We would paint the third bedroom, made a guestroom.
One to three years. Feeding tube recommended.
They call him the patient.

2.

Too short of breath to light cigarettes,
he blew on the ember with an oxygen cannula
until things caught. No sense quitting now.

Mom at three packs a day. Mom at home
in robe and house slippers, three in the afternoon,
too busy with him to dress. He in pain, almost finished.

3.

He instructs me to leave the room *when*.
Only mom here he says. *Your mother* he calls her.
Things that are absurd (a list):

The way TV continues while someone dies.
How we migrate to familiar programming.
The strange comfort of predictable distraction.

The way Spring broadcasts herself all over the patio;
light entering, laying bare the corners of rooms.
Laying bare his final face: Startled and unpeaceful.

Update to Dad

november second

Today would have been your birthday. Fifty-nine.
You have a grandson who looks like you.

It is rainy autumn day,
everything your last day in spring wasn't.

I've learned to love this mist and grayness,
this grief.

There is thunder
and the fat drops falling so fast.

Note to Heart

My God, you've dragged this ache around like
hunger for a cycle of seasons, as if
afraid to unhand it. Look,

snow out one window, sunshine pouring in
the other. Trillium and trout lily and snow flurries.
Give it up. Let one season wrench away

the next. It's time to choose sun
heating the right side of the body,
alighting the jar of paper clips in the window sill

rendering the familiar warmth of misery
and this hissing space heater
unessential and annoying.

Thirst

I get out of the tub, see past the bedroom door
stacks of folded laundry all over the table

and by the window, clothes hung to dry and also
five coats strewn over a chair back

whose cover is stained
and instead of domesticity sucking me into

hopelessness and because
I've managed a few poems and a bath

while the baby naps and I slept well
and last night listened to a poet

who is no longer afraid of happiness, who
no longer waits for bad news to click

into place where dread has been.
I look at all the mess and think

I want a glass of water.
And I have one.

Happy Dog Poem

So, it's here now, after a season
of biting cold and bleak metaphors and
before the season of excess, frenzied stinging
insects and mosquito-laden pools.
A spring day—trout lilies and
spring beauties and a brilliant moss over
the rocks; a day the dog runs up the trail
through the woods toward you—the aroma of
the bloated rabbit corpse he just wallowed in
arriving before him. He is dog-happy. He
shakes lavishly and droplets fly from his black fur
like sparks from a dark nightgown
and now you know—this is the day
to unhand darkness.

Late Spring

Finally, the splintered oak has leafed out,
the tender greens raw
with beginning.

I remember you turning away
this morning, not angry exactly
or sad exactly, but something between us

still unnamed,
something our words pause around,
something fragile and deserving of patience.

Understanding

The perched birds, crying and unseen among the branches,
come into view and I realize for the first time
how their resting bodies resemble leaves
and that this is why the eye is slow to notice.

And it seems the trees are filled with birds
and that there are no leaves at all and soon
all their wings will fly open at once
and our eyes will know how wrong they've been.

Error

Yesterday, anger was a sanctuary
from that which is good and true and terrifying .

This morning clouds hang low over the water
and the sky is a shocking state of blue.

The clouds have fallen
and the truth is the blue that was always there.

Last Sunday of May, Pediatric I.C.U.

I see the woman rocking and what I think is *another one*.
Another mother. Another rocking chair. Another dying child.
And a flock of family clamoring at the door to watch.
Liver failure, kidney failure, brain failure.

I enter the room, make adjustments, make myself busy,
mix and check infusions that drip into cannulated veins,
measure amber urine that coils along a plastic catheter.
A mechanical click and swish, a chest rising. Nothing.

The mother sees stumbling green peaks of heartbeats
and like parents here before her, hangs everything
on this tracing that levels every few beats
although she hasn't noticed this yet.

I want to tell her the heart is a stupid organ,
not knowing when to quit. Instead
I do the medical tasks, do not shout, as I should
that he is dead and all of this the lie.

It will be a long day. A day without the shouting of realities.
One of quiet talk and this woman telling again and again
and my hearing a story not meant for me,
a story that will spiral her into what waits.

She put the baby down for sleep, left him alone,
went to fold laundry. She smoothed warm towels over
and across, stacked them in satisfying rows,
her hands still warm when she returned to the infant

who was cool and blue in the crib.
She remembers what waits at home, first
the stacked towels, long-cooled,
then those walks from one room to another.

Hospital Smoker

She holds the smoke in,
attends it
like a wound.

The release
reluctant and slow
like the letting go of the beloved.

The slow sweep of arm—
an embrace of bleakness, a beckoning
of numbness

and in that moment between exhalation
and the hand's deliberate return,
ruin shines on her face.

Mercy

Unsanctioned and
perhaps holy among the brambles
lies the small patch of trillium nearly
trod upon, saved unconsciously
by peripheral vision—a golden glint
perceived without intent
or even goodwill.

Lyme Disease

You are swollen and aching and pumped
with antibiotics and now each evening
we hunt our bodies, rid ourselves of lurking deer ticks .

They don't just drink their fill and go like mosquitoes
but cling disgustingly, gorge again
and again.

They refuse to go to bed, demand
another glass of water and are by the bed when we wake
saying "I'm hungry."

Two Walls Painted

The man outside hanging boards on a house,
cigarette loose between his lips,
the sleeping child who has nested himself in a circle of toys
and a woman painting an old room.

It is the second day of spring. Two walls
have a new layer of Antique White # 8904.
It is lovely simple labor with the breeze now and then
through the open window, touching all of us just the same.

Carolyn Welch worked for many years as a pediatric intensive care nurse, all the while writing poetry and short fiction. She has an MFA from the Bennington Writing Seminars. She currently works as a family nurse practitioner and occasionally teaches community-based writing classes. Carolyn's poetry and fiction have appeared in *Gulf Coast, Poet Lore, Sundog, Tar River Poetry, Conduit, Connecticut River Review, High Desert Journal, The Southeast Review, Zone 3, The Minnesota Review, American Journal of Nursing* and other literary journals. Her poem "Rain Run" was nominated for a Pushcart. She lives in Tennessee with her husband, children and three spoiled rescue dogs.